MEATMEN

COOKING CHANNEL

ZI CHAR AT HOME

HEARTY HOME-STYLE SINGAPOREAN DISHES

mc Marshall Cavendish
Cuisine

All photographs by TheMeatMen Channel Pte Ltd except for those on pages
1–4, 6–11, 14–15, 32–33, 54–55, 74–75, 80–81, 88 and the back cover

Editor: Lydia Leong
Designer: Bernard Go Kwang Meng

Published by Marshall Cavendish Cuisine
An imprint of Marshall Cavendish International

A member of the
Times Publishing Group

Other Marshall Cavendish Offices:
Marshall Cavendish Corporation, 99 White Plains Road, Tarrytown NY
10591-9001, USA • Marshall Cavendish International (Thailand) Co Ltd.
253 Asoke, 12th Flr, Sukhumvit 21 Road, Klongtoey Nua, Wattana,
Bangkok 10110, Thailand • Marshall Cavendish (Malaysia) Sdn Bhd,
Times Subang, Lot 46, Subang Hi-Tech Industrial Park, Batu Tiga,
40000 Shah Alam, Selangor Darul Ehsan, Malaysia.

Marshall Cavendish is a registered trademark of Times Publishing Limited

National Library Board, Singapore Cataloguing-in-Publication Data

Name(s): MeatMen Cooking Channel.
Title: MeatMen Cooking Channel zi char at home : hearty home-style
Singaporean dishes / Meatmen.
Other titles: Hearty home-style Singaporean dishes
Description: Singapore : Marshall Cavendish Cuisine, [2017]
Identifier(s): OCN 962466337 | ISBN 978-981-47-5164-3 (paperback)
Subject(s): LCSH: Cooking, Singaporean. | Cooking, Chinese. | Cookbooks.
Classification: DDC 641.595957--dc23

Printed by Times Offset (M) Sdn Bhd

DEDICATION

This book is dedicated to the pioneers of Asian food culture — the *zi char* chefs who work tirelessly every day to refine their craft. It is from their passion that our cooking channel is given life.

We would also like to dedicate this book to our fans on social media and beyond, for their support and encouragement all these years.

CONTENTS

ACKNOWLEDGEMENTS

As with our first book, *MeatMen Cooking Channel: Hawker Favourites*, this second book would not have been possible without the support of many people.

Thanks to the team at Marshall Cavendish International (Asia) for believing in us.

We are also grateful to our loved ones for their continued understanding and encouragement.

Last but not least, many thanks to our FANS, for their constant support in allowing us to pursue our passion of developing recipes for them. We sincerely hope that this book will bring yet more happy surprises for them as they continue in their cooking journey.

The MeatMen Cooking Channel

INTRODUCTION

Zi char (煮炒) is a term used to refer to Chinese food stalls that offer on their menus a plethora of home-styled dishes that can be made-to-order based on the taste requirements of diners.

Just as hawker food is something that we have grown up with in Singapore, *zi char* food is also close to our hearts and forms a large part of our food heritage. *Zi char* dishes are hearty, delicious and affordable, and we have worked hard to capture the goodness of these dishes in our recipes, to encourage people all over to enjoy *zi char* cuisine the way we do.

It is our hope that you will enjoy the process of preparing and cooking these dishes at home to share with your families and loved ones.

Enjoy!

ABOUT THE MEATMEN COOKING CHANNEL

We are simply a bunch of greedy guys in the creative trade who love their food, be it eating, cooking, growing or even capturing it on film.

It all started with the obsession to record the whole process of food creation through the lens. That passion soon spread and before long, we were infected with the food-frenzy craze.

We are about being simple. Our vision is simple, to prove that cooking at home is not difficult. We hope to simplify it for everyone to make cooking easy and fun for all.

The MeatMen Cooking Channel symbolises a vision we have to bring awesome local dish dishes from hawker centres and coffee shops to the comfort of our own homes.

Chris Lim

Kiat Yingda

Tan Junjie

Jonathan Tan

MEAT AND POULTRY

The local name of this dish, *pai gu wang*, translates literally to pork rib KING.
When a dish is so named, it can only mean that it is that good! And our recipe is
definitely worthy of that title. Most *zi char* stalls use pork chops when preparing this dish.
We use a meaty cut of pork ribs known as pork loin back ribs.

PORK RIB KING

Serves 4

700 g (1½ lb) pork loin
  back ribs

1 Tbsp sesame oil

2 tsp salt

½ tsp ground white pepper

1 Tbsp ginger paste (made by
  blending ginger with water)

1 Tbsp rice wine

1 Tbsp oyster sauce

½ tsp baking soda

1 egg, beaten

2 Tbsp custard powder

2 Tbsp potato starch

Cooking oil for deep-frying

2 Tbsp white sesame seeds,
  toasted

1 sprig coriander leaves
  (cilantro)

SAUCE

3 Tbsp sugar

3 Tbsp brown sugar

2 Tbsp rice vinegar

100 ml (3½ fl oz) water

2 Tbsp tomato ketchup

1 Tbsp plum sauce

1 tsp Worcestershire sauce

1 Tbsp brown sauce

1 Tbsp steak sauce

1 Tbsp cornflour, mixed
  with 2 Tbsp water

1 tsp dark soy sauce

1. Cut ribs into individual pieces and tenderise with
   a meat tenderiser.

2. Place ribs in a large bowl and add sesame oil, salt,
   pepper, ginger paste, rice wine, oyster sauce and
   baking soda. Mix well.

3. Add egg, custard powder and potato starch and
   mix again. Cover bowl and set aside to marinate
   for 1 hour.

4. Combine all ingredients for sauce in another bowl
   and mix well. Set aside.

5. Heat sufficient oil for deep-frying in a wok over
   medium heat. Gently lower marinated ribs into
   hot oil and deep-fry until golden brown. Drain well
   and set aside.

6. Drain oil from wok and reheat wok over medium heat.
   Add sauce to wok and let cook until sauce starts
   to thicken.

7. Return fried ribs to wok and mix to coat ribs well
   with sauce.

8. Dish out and garnish with toasted sesame seeds
   and coriander leaves. Serve.

Coffee and pork ribs. Who would have thought that such an unlikely pairing would taste so darn good! This awesome coffee-flavoured dish works best with a good cut of pork ribs. Use our recipe to whip up a meaty to-die-for dish that's crisp on the outside, yet so juicy on the inside.

COFFEE PORK RIBS

Serves 4

500 g (1 lb 1¹/₂ oz) pork ribs
¹/₂ tsp salt
¹/₂ tsp sugar
2 Tbsp oyster sauce
1 tsp sesame oil
¹/₂ tsp baking soda
2 Tbsp rice flour
2 Tbsp potato starch
3 Tbsp water
1 egg, beaten
Cooking oil for deep-frying
1 bird's eye chilli (*cili padi*), sliced
1 sprig coriander leaves (cilantro)

SAUCE

2 sachets 3-in-1 instant coffee
1 Tbsp brown sugar
1 Tbsp sugar
1 Tbsp minced garlic
2 Tbsp Worcestershire sauce
1 Tbsp rice wine (optional)
1 Tbsp dark soy sauce
3 Tbsp water

1. Cut ribs into individual pieces.

2. Place ribs in a large bowl and add salt, sugar, oyster sauce, sesame oil, baking soda, rice flour, potato starch, water and egg. Mix well. Cover bowl and set aside to marinate for 1 hour.

3. Combine all ingredients for sauce in another bowl and mix well. Set aside.

4. Heat sufficient oil for deep-frying in a wok over medium heat. Gently lower marinated ribs into hot oil and deep-fry until golden brown. Drain well and set aside.

5. Drain oil from wok and reheat wok over medium heat. Add sauce to wok and let cook until sauce starts to thicken.

6. Return fried ribs to wok and mix to coat ribs well with sauce.

7. Dish out and garnish with bird's eye chilli and coriander leaves. Serve.

Another awesome pork rib dish with bold flavours! If you love stout, look no further! When making this dish, we start by frying the pork ribs to crispy perfection on the outside, while the inside stays moist and juicy. The use of stout in both the marinade and sauce gives the ribs "body" while also imparting a slight bitterness to it.

PORK RIBS WITH STOUT

Serves 4

600 g (1 lb 5$\frac{1}{3}$ oz) pork ribs
2 Tbsp tapioca starch
Cooking oil for deep-frying

MARINADE
100 ml (3$\frac{1}{2}$ fl oz) stout
2 Tbsp oyster sauce
1 Tbsp light soy sauce
1 tsp sugar
$\frac{1}{2}$ tsp ground white pepper
$\frac{1}{2}$ tsp salt

SAUCE
250 ml (8 fl oz / 1 cup) stout
2 Tbsp light soy sauce
2 Tbsp oyster sauce
2 Tbsp tomato ketchup
1 Tbsp sugar

1. Cut ribs into individual pieces.

2. Place ribs in a large bowl and add ingredients for marinade. Mix well. Cover bowl and set aside to marinate for at least 1 hour.

3. When ready to cook ribs, add tapioca starch to ribs and mix well.

4. Heat sufficient oil for deep-frying in a wok over medium heat. Gently lower marinated ribs into hot oil and deep-fry until golden brown. Drain well and set aside.

5. Drain oil from wok and reheat wok over medium heat. Mix ingredients for sauce in a bowl and add to wok. Let cook until sauce starts to thicken.

6. Return fried ribs to wok and mix to coat ribs well with sauce.

7. Dish out, garnish as desired and serve.

We all *LOVE* deep-fried stuff and who can resist it? Another *zi char* classic,
this dish of deep-fried crispy pork chops coated with a rich and buttery sauce,
infused with curry leaves, is something we can't say no to!

BUTTER PORK CHOPS

Serves 4

600 g (1 lb 5¹/₃ oz) pork
 chops, each about 1-cm
 (¹/₂-in) thick

Cooking oil for deep-frying

MARINADE

¹/₂ tsp baking soda

1 tsp salt

1 Tbsp sugar

¹/₂ tsp ground white pepper

1 tsp sesame oil

1 Tbsp light soy sauce

1 Tbsp Chinese rice wine
 (*hua tiao jiu*) (optional)

1 egg white

1 Tbsp cornflour

BUTTER SAUCE

1 Tbsp cooking oil

1 Tbsp minced garlic

50 g (1³/₄ oz) butter

20 curry leaves

85 ml (2¹/₂ fl oz) evaporated
 milk

2 Tbsp cooking cream

¹/₄ tsp chicken seasoning
 powder

¹/₂ tsp sugar

¹/₄ tsp ground white pepper

2 bird's eye chillies (*cili padi*),
 sliced

1. Place pork chops in a bowl. Add ingredients
 for marinade and mix well. Cover bowl and
 set aside to marinate for 1 hour.

2. Heat sufficient oil for deep-frying in a wok over
 medium heat, and deep-fry marinated pork chops
 until golden brown. Drain well and set aside.

3. Drain oil from wok and reheat wok over
 medium heat.

4. Prepare butter sauce. Add oil to wok and when hot,
 add minced garlic, butter, curry leaves, evaporated
 milk and cooking cream. Bring to a boil and let
 cook until sauce is slightly thickened. Add chicken
 seasoning powder, sugar, pepper and bird's eye
 chillies. Mix well.

5. Return fried pork chops to wok and mix to coat
 pork chops well with sauce. Dish out and serve.

Har cheong gai, fried chicken marinated with fine shrimp paste,
is one *zi char* dish that EVERYONE who has ever tried it loves. And we are
extremely proud of our recipe for this hot favourite. It's definitely AS GOOD AS
those you get from the *zi char* stalls, or even better! We kid you not!

HAR CHEONG GAI PRAWN PASTE CHICKEN

Serves 4

12 chicken mid-joint wings

Cooking oil for deep-frying

MARINADE

2 Tbsp fine shrimp sauce

1 Tbsp sugar

1 Tbsp sesame oil

2 Tbsp Chinese rice wine
(*hua tiao jiu*) (optional)

1 Tbsp oyster sauce

1/2 tsp ground white pepper

BATTER

6 Tbsp plain flour

6 Tbsp potato starch

1/4 tsp baking powder

1 egg, beaten

50 ml (1²/₃ fl oz) water

1. Place chicken mid-joint wings in a bowl. Add ingredients for marinade and mix well. Transfer wings to a resealable plastic bag, seal and place in the refrigerator to marinate for at least 4 hours.

2. Prepare batter. Combine ingredients for batter and mix until batter is smooth.

3. Add marinated wings to batter and mix well.

4. Heat sufficient oil for deep-frying in a wok over medium heat. Add wings and deep-fry until golden brown. Keep oil at 180°C (350°F) while frying wings.

5. Wings will start to float in 4–5 minutes when they are done. Remove and drain well. Serve.

We call this the kick-ass *zi char* version of popcorn chicken — chunks of juicy chicken thigh meat deep-fried and coated with a mouth-watering butter and salted egg yolk sauce, finished with fiery bird's eye chilli and fragrant curry leaves.

SALTED EGG YOLK CHICKEN

Serves 4

2 boneless chicken thighs (with or without skin, depending on preference)

1 egg, beaten

170 g (5²/₃ oz) potato starch

Cooking oil as needed

2–3 bird's eye chillies (*cili padi*), sliced

20 curry leaves

20 g (²/₃ oz) butter

MARINADE

1 tsp sugar

¹/₂ tsp salt

¹/₄ tsp ground white pepper

1 Tbsp rice wine

SALTED EGG YOLK SAUCE

2 salted egg yolks

1 Tbsp cooking oil

¹/₂ tsp minced garlic

¹/₂ tsp minced ginger

1. Cut chicken thighs into 3-cm (1-in) chunks.

2. Place chicken chunks in a bowl and add ingredients for marinade. Mix well. Cover and set aside to marinate for 15 minutes.

3. In the meantime, prepare salted egg yolk sauce. Steam salted egg yolks for 10 minutes, then mash as fine as possible.

4. Heat oil in a pan over medium heat. Add mashed salted egg yolks and stir-fry until foamy. Add minced garlic and minced ginger and stir-fry until fragrant. Dish out and set aside.

5. Add beaten egg to marinated chicken chunks and mix well.

6. Spread potato starch out on a tray and coat chicken chunks evenly with potato starch.

7. Heat sufficient oil for deep-frying in a wok over medium heat. When oil is 160°C (325°F), add chicken chunks and deep-fry until golden brown. Drain well and set aside.

8. Heat 1 Tbsp oil in a clean pan over medium heat. Add bird's eye chillies and curry leaves. Stir-fry lightly, then add butter and half the salted egg yolk sauce. Stir-fry until fragrant.

9. Add fried chicken chunks and toss until evenly coated with sauce. Dish out and serve.

Infusing the oil with peppercorns and dried chillies gives this dish its distinctive *kung pao* chicken kick! Adding loads of aromatics like ginger, garlic and spring onions makes the dish even more appetising. We use chicken thigh meat over breast meat so that it stays juicy even after cooking. This is a great dish to enjoy with piping hot rice!

KUNG PAO CHICKEN

Serves 4

3 boneless chicken thighs (with or without skin, depending on preference)

5 Tbsp cooking oil

1 Tbsp black/Sichuan peppercorns

15 dried chillies, seeds removed

3 cloves garlic, peeled and sliced

1 Tbsp chopped ginger

4 spring onions (scallions), cut into 5-cm (2-in) lengths

5-cm (2-in) knob ginger, peeled and sliced

2 bird's eye chillies (*cili padi*), sliced

1 Tbsp dark soy sauce

MARINADE

1 Tbsp light soy sauce

1 Tbsp Chinese rice wine (*hua tiao jiu*)

$1/2$ tsp salt

2 tsp cornflour

SAUCE

2 Tbsp rice vinegar

1 Tbsp light soy sauce

2 Tbsp water

2 Tbsp sugar

1. Cut chicken thighs into chunks about 3-cm ($1^1/_5$-in) each.

2. Place chicken chunks in a bowl and add ingredients for marinade. Mix well. Cover and set aside to marinate for 30 minutes.

3. Combine ingredients for sauce in a small bowl. Mix well and set aside.

4. Heat 3 Tbsp oil in a wok over medium heat. Add black/Sichuan peppercorns and stir-fry until fragrant. Remove peppercorns and set aside.

5. In the same wok, stir-fry dried chillies until darkened. Add garlic, ginger and a third of spring onions. Stir-fry until fragrant.

6. Add sauce and cook for 2 minutes. Transfer to a bowl and set sauce aside.

7. Add 2 Tbsp oil to wok and stir-fry ginger, bird's eye chillies and remaining spring onions until fragrant.

8. Add marinated chicken chunks and stir-fry until chicken is almost done. Add sauce and dark soy sauce. Stir-fry to mix and cook for another minute until chicken is done.

9. Dish out and garnish as desired. Serve.

Lemon chicken is a classic dish that was wildly popular decades ago.
Good old crispy fried chicken coated with a sweet and tangy sauce,
oozing with the fresh scent of lemons — what is there not to like?

LEMON CHICKEN CHOP

Serves 4

3 boneless chicken thighs
(with or without skin,
depending on preference)

170 g (5²/₃ oz) potato starch

Cooking oil for deep-frying

MARINADE

1 Tbsp light soy sauce

¹/₂ tsp salt

¹/₄ tsp ground white pepper

1 Tbsp sesame oil

1 egg white

SAUCE

1 Tbsp cooking oil

¹/₂ medium onion, peeled
and sliced

125 ml (4 fl oz / ¹/₂ cup) water

3 Tbsp plum sauce

Juice from 1 medium lemon

¹/₂ medium lemon, thinly
sliced

1. Place chicken thighs in a bowl and add ingredients
   for marinade. Mix well. Cover bowl and set aside to
   marinate for at least 30 minutes.

2. Spread potato starch out on a tray and coat
   marinated chicken thighs evenly with potato starch.

3. Heat sufficient oil for deep-frying in a wok over
   medium heat. When oil is 180°C (350°F), add
   chicken thighs and deep-fry until golden brown.
   Drain well and set aside.

4. Prepare sauce. Heat oil in a wok over medium heat.
   Add onion and stir-fry until softened. Add water,
   plum sauce, lemon juice and lemon slices. Mix well
   and cook until sauce thickens.

5. Cut fried chicken thighs into strips and arrange on
   a serving plate. Drizzle sauce over chicken. Garnish
   as desired and serve.

FISH AND SEAFOOD

This is a delicious, thick soup that we have all grown up loving. To start off, soak and cut the fish maw, then bring to a boil. The mushrooms and sauces give the soup a wonderful flavour, while the cornflour helps to thicken it and gives it the texture that makes it so satisfying.

FISH MAW SOUP

Serves 4

40 g (1¹⁄₃ oz) fish maw

3 dried shiitake mushrooms

250 ml (8 fl oz / 1 cup) water

250 ml (8 fl oz / 1 cup)
  chicken stock

200 g (7 oz) crabmeat

2 Tbsp oyster sauce,
  or to taste

2 Tbsp abalone sauce,
  or to taste

1 tsp sesame oil

¹⁄₂ tsp salt, or to taste

¹⁄₄ tsp ground white pepper

1 tsp light soy sauce

1 Tbsp Chinese rice wine
  (*hua tiao jiu*)

3–4 Tbsp cornflour mixture
  (made using a ratio of
  1 Tbsp cornflour to
  2 Tbsp water)

2 Tbsp Chinese black vinegar
  (optional)

1 sprig coriander leaves
  (cilantro)

1. Soak fish maw and mushrooms separately in hot water until softened. Squeeze water from fish maw and cut into 2.5-cm (1-in) pieces. Trim stems from mushrooms and discard. Slice caps into strips. Set aside.

2. Combine water and chicken stock in a wok and bring to a boil. Add fish maw and simmer over low heat for 10 minutes.

3. Add mushrooms and crabmeat, then season with oyster sauce, abalone sauce, sesame oil, salt, pepper, light soy sauce and Chinese rice wine. Bring to a boil and let cook for 5 minutes.

4. Add 3–4 Tbsp cornflour mixture and stir until soup thickens slightly.

5. Dish out into individual serving bowls. Drizzle with black vinegar, if desired, and garnish with coriander leaves. Serve.

The key to a good fish or seafood dish is in the freshness of the ingredients. When choosing fish, ensure that the eyes look bright, and are clear and convex. There should be no strong smell, the gills should be bright red and the belly firm, not swollen or sunken.

STEAMED FISH, CANTONESE-STYLE

Serves 4

1 small sea bass, cleaned

3 spring onions (scallions)

40 g (1⅓ oz) ginger, peeled

¼ tsp salt

¼ tsp ground white pepper

2 Tbsp Chinese rice wine (*hua tiao jiu*)

3 Tbsp peanut oil

Coriander leaves (cilantro)

SAUCE

3 Tbsp light soy sauce

1 Tbsp rock sugar

1 Tbsp brown sugar

½ tsp ground white pepper

1 Tbsp sesame oil

4 Tbsp water

1. Rinse fish well and set aside.

2. Cut green leaves of spring onions into 5-cm (2-in) lengths and white part into strips.

3. Cut half the ginger into slices and the remaining half into strips.

4. Season inside and outside of fish with salt and pepper. Place on a steaming plate. Drizzle fish with Chinese rice wine and stuff with sliced ginger. Place white part of spring onions under fish.

5. Steam fish for 7–9 minutes or until done. The cooking time will depend on the size of the fish.

6. Combine ingredients for sauce in a bowl and mix well.

7. When fish is done, remove from steamer and pour sauce over fish. Top with ginger strips and green part of spring onions.

8. Heat 3 Tbsp peanut oil in a pan until it is sizzling hot. Drizzle hot oil over fish.

9. Garnish fish with coriander and serve.

This dish is a favourite at many *zi char* stalls in Singapore. Most people love eating this and so do we, for the simple reason that they're so sinfully satisfying! There's just something special about deep-fried prawns coated in butter and cereal.

CEREAL PRAWNS

Serves 4

12 large prawns

1/2 egg, beaten

2 tsp salt

1 tsp ground white pepper

1 Tbsp plain flour

1 Tbsp cornflour

Cooking oil for deep-frying

60 g (2 oz) instant cereal

1 Tbsp milk powder

1 Tbsp sugar

1 tsp chicken seasoning powder

50 g (1 3/4 oz) unsalted butter

20 curry leaves

4 bird's eye chillies (*cili padi*), chopped

1. Clean prawns. Trim legs and devein, leaving heads and shells on. Place prawns in a bowl.

2. Add beaten egg to prawns and coat evenly.

3. Add 1/2 tsp salt, pepper, plain flour and cornflour to prawns and mix well.

4. Heat sufficient oil for deep-frying in a wok. When oil is 170°C (330°F), add prawns and deep-fry for 2–3 minutes until golden brown. Drain well and set aside.

5. Combine instant cereal, milk powder, sugar, chicken seasoning powder and 1 tsp salt in a bowl. Mix evenly.

6. Melt butter in a pan over medium heat. Add curry leaves and chillies, and stir-fry lightly.

7. Add cereal mixture and stir-fry over medium-low heat. Mix well.

8. Add fried prawns and mix well. Dish out and serve.

A simple dish that everyone can cook and which doesn't take up a chunk of your time. The key to this dish is FRESHNESS. Try to use sea prawns as they definitely taste better than the farmed ones. It is also advisable to get large prawns so you're less likely to overcook them during the steaming process!

STEAMED GARLIC PRAWNS

Serves 4

12 large prawns

1 spring onion (scallion), finely chopped

GARLIC SAUCE

4 Tbsp chicken stock

1 Tbsp light soy sauce

1 Tbsp Chinese rice wine (*hua tiao jiu*) (optional)

1 Tbsp sesame oil

$^1/_2$ tsp salt

1 Tbsp minced ginger

2 Tbsp minced garlic

1 spring onion (scallion), chopped

1. Combine all ingredients for garlic sauce in a bowl. Mix well and set aside.

2. Clean and trim prawns, leaving heads and shells on. Make a slit down the back of each prawn and devein.

3. Arrange prawns side by side on a steaming tray with the slit side up.

4. Pour garlic sauce over prawns and steam for 4–5 minutes until prawns change colour and are done. The cooking time will depend on the size of the prawns.

5. When prawns are done, remove from steamer and top with chopped spring onion. Serve.

We may not have thought about it, but the part of the scallop that is usually consumed is the large adductor muscle. In this dish, broccoli may seem like it's playing second fiddle, BUT don't underestimate its role. The crunchy stems and tender florets take up the abalone sauce and offer a flavourful textural contrast to the scallops.

SCALLOP AND BROCCOLI WITH ABALONE SAUCE

Serves 4

1 litre (32 fl oz / 4 cups) water

1 Tbsp salt

2 small heads broccoli, cut into bite-size pieces

500 g (1 lb 1½ oz) scallops

SAUCE

125 ml (8 fl oz / ½ cup) water

3 Tbsp abalone sauce

2 Tbsp oyster sauce

1–2 tsp light soy sauce

1 Tbsp Chinese rice wine (*hua tiao jiu*)

1 tsp sugar

1 Tbsp cornflour, mixed with 2 Tbsp water

1. Bring water and salt to a boil in a wok. Add broccoli to boiling water and blanch for 5 minutes. Remove with a strainer and plunge into a basin of iced water. Drain well. Arrange broccoli on a serving plate. Set aside.

2. Return water to the boil and blanch scallops for 3–4 minutes until lightly cooked. The cooking time will depend on the size of the scallops. Drain and arrange with broccoli on the serving plate.

3. Prepare sauce. Heat water in a wok over medium heat. Add abalone sauce, oyster sauce, light soy sauce, Chinese rice wine and sugar. Mix well and bring to a boil. Lower heat and add cornflour mixture. Stir until sauce thickens.

4. Pour sauce over scallops and broccoli. Serve.

What's better than a dish of squid? A dish of *baby* squid of course!
Baby squid are bite-sized, so you can enjoy the full FLAVOUR of a whole squid
with every mouthful. And that's not all. These babies are deep-fried and coated with
a delightful honey and soy sauce, making every bite an acute pleasure!

DEEP-FRIED BABY SQUID WITH HONEY

Serves 4

140 g (5 oz) rice flour

1 tsp salt

1 tsp ground white pepper

1 kg (2 lb 3 oz) baby squid

Cooking oil for deep-frying

SAUCE

125 ml (4 fl oz / $1/2$ cup) water

85 g (3 oz) honey

2 Tbsp light soy sauce

$1/2$ tsp dark soy sauce

$1/2$ tsp salt

1. Combine rice flour, salt and pepper in a bowl. Mix well and add baby squid. Coat evenly.

2. Heat sufficient oil for deep-frying in a wok over medium heat. Add baby squid and deep-fry until golden brown. Drain well and set aside.

3. Prepare sauce. Heat water in a clean wok over medium heat. Add honey, soy sauces and salt. Mix well and simmer until sauce thickens.

4. Add fried baby squid and toss until squid is evenly coated with sauce.

5. Dish out and serve.

This is a popular dish that can be found at most food stalls selling *nasi padang* and/or *nasi lemak*. And all it takes is fresh squid (or sotong) with a good sambal. If you like squid and spicy food, this dish is for you!

SAMBAL SOTONG

Serves 4

1 kg (2 lb 3 oz) squid (sotong)

2 Tbsp cooking oil

1 medium onion, peeled
   and sliced

2 tomatoes, cut into wedges

50 ml (1²/₃ fl oz) water

1 Tbsp sugar

1 tsp salt

6 calamansi limes, halved

SAMBAL

20 g (²/₃ oz) dried chillies

20 g (²/₃ oz) *belacan*
   (dried prawn paste)

80 g (2⁴/₅ oz) red chillies

150 g (5¹/₃ oz) shallots,
   peeled

60 g (2 oz) garlic, peeled

40 g (1¹/₃ oz) lemongrass,
   ends trimmed and sliced

25 g (⁴/₅ oz) ginger, peeled

40 g (1¹/₃ oz) palm sugar

2 Tbsp tamarind pulp,
   mixed with 3 Tbsp
   hot water and strained

100 ml (3¹/₂ fl oz) cooking oil

1. Prepare sambal. Remove seeds from dried chillies, then soak dried chillies in hot water for 30 minutes or until softened. Dry-fry *belacan* in a pan, breaking it up until fragrant and dry.

2. Place red chillies, dried chillies, shallots, garlic, lemongrass, ginger, toasted dried prawn paste, palm sugar and tamarind liquid in a food processor. Blend into a smooth paste.

3. Heat 100 ml (3¹/₂ fl oz) oil in a pan over medium heat. Add sambal paste and salt and stir-fry until mixture is fragrant and oil starts to separate. Remove and set aside.

4. Clean squid. Twist and remove squid heads from bodies. The entrails should follow. Trim ink sacs and beaks from tentacles and discard. Rinse tentacles and set aside. Peel skin from squid tubes. Rinse and slice squid tubes into 1-cm (¹/₂-in) rings.

5. Heat 2 Tbsp oil in a clean wok over medium heat. Add onion and tomatoes. Stir-fry lightly, then add sambal paste, water, sugar and salt. Mix well and bring to a boil.

6. Add squid, cover wok and let cook for 6–8 minutes or until squid is just done. Dish out and serve with calamansi limes on the side.

This classic dish is often found on the menus of Chinese restaurants the world over. Each restaurant will have its own recipe for this dish, but oyster sauce and soy sauce are standard ingredients. It's a simple dish to make and a great choice for Chinese New Year reunion dinners and other celebratory occasions.

BRAISED ABALONE WITH MUSHROOMS

Serves 6

1 litre (32 fl oz / 4 cups) chicken stock

20 g (^{2}/$_3$ oz) *jin hua* ham, cut into small cubes

2 Tbsp abalone sauce

1 Tbsp oyster sauce

^{1}/$_4$ tsp dark soy sauce

2 Tbsp Chinese rice wine (*hua tiao jiu*)

24 baby abalone, cleaned

8 dried shiitake mushrooms, soaked in hot water until softened, stems trimmed

1 tsp salt

1 Tbsp cooking oil

150 g (5^1/$_3$ oz) baby bok choy

SAUCE

100 ml (3^1/$_2$ fl oz) water

1 tsp sugar

2–3 Tbsp cornflour mixture (made using a ratio of 1 Tbsp cornflour to 2 Tbsp water)

1. Place chicken stock in a pressure cooker. Add *jin hua* ham, abalone sauce, oyster sauce, dark soy sauce and Chinese rice wine, followed by abalone and mushrooms. Cover and turn on pressure cooker to cook for 15–20 minutes. Alternatively, cook in a clay pot or slow cooker for 2–3 hours until abalone is tender.

2. In the meantime, bring a pot of water to the boil. Add salt and oil, then blanch baby bok choy for 2–3 minutes. Drain baby bok choy and arrange on a serving plate.

3. Arrange braised mushrooms and abalone over baby bok choy.

4. Prepare sauce. Combine 100 ml (3^1/$_2$ fl oz) water, 100 ml (3^1/$_2$ fl oz) braising liquid from pressure cooker and sugar in a wok. Bring to a boil, then lower heat and add cornflour mixture. Stir until sauce thickens. Pour sauce over dish and serve.

This is a super simple, yet really satisfying dish that you can whip up in 10 minutes! We kid you not! All it takes is to stir-fry the clams (also known as *lala*) with ginger, garlic and bird's eye chillies, then finish it off with a splash of Chinese rice wine in the hot wok!

STIR-FRIED CLAMS

Serves 4

2 Tbsp cooking oil

1 Tbsp minced ginger

1 Tbsp minced garlic

2 bird's eye chillies (*cili padi*), sliced

600 g (1 lb 5$\frac{1}{3}$ oz) clams, cleaned

1 Tbsp sesame oil

2 Tbsp light soy sauce

2 Tbsp Chinese rice wine (*hua tiao jiu*)

$\frac{1}{2}$ tsp salt

$\frac{1}{2}$ tsp sugar

4 Tbsp water

2 spring onions (scallions), chopped

1. Heat oil in a wok over medium heat. Add minced ginger, minced garlic and chillies. Stir-fry until fragrant.

2. Add clams and season with sesame oil, light soy sauce, Chinese rice wine, salt and sugar. Stir-fry and mix well.

3. Add water and turn heat up to high. Cover wok and let cook for 30 seconds until clams open. Discard any that do not open.

4. Dish out and garnish with chopped spring onions. Serve.

The marvellous things one can do with *you tiao!* A sinfully scrumptious
deep-fried *zi char* favourite, the squid and prawn paste is what sets this dish apart.
Don't forget to add the floss for that final touch!

DEEP-FRIED STUFFED YOU TIAO

Serves 4

150 g (5¹/₃ oz) squid

150 g (5¹/₃ oz) prawns,
  peeled and deveined

1 tsp sesame oil

1 tsp salt

1 tsp sugar

1 tsp Chinese rice wine
  (*hua tiao jiu*)

1 egg white

1 Tbsp cornflour

3 sticks *you tiao*
  (Chinese crullers)

Cooking oil for deep-frying

4–5 Tbsp chicken/pork floss

Mayonnaise (optional)

1. Clean squid. Twist and remove heads from bodies. The entrails should follow. Trim ink sacs and beaks from tentacles and discard. Rinse tentacles and set aside. Peel skin from squid tubes. Rinse and slice into rings.

2. Place squid, prawns, sesame oil, salt, sugar, Chinese rice wine, egg white and cornflour in a food processor and blend into a smooth paste.

3. Cut *you tiao* into 5-cm (2-in) lengths and make a slit in the centre of each piece. Spoon paste into *you tiao*.

4. Heat sufficient oil for deep-frying in a wok over medium heat. Add stuffed *you tiao* and deep-fry for 6–8 minutes or until gold brown. Remove and drain well.

5. Sprinkle fried *you tiao* with chicken/pork floss. Serve with mayonnaise on the side if desired.

VEGETABLES, EGGS AND TOFU

This dish combines not two, but THREE types of eggs with chicken stock for that ultimate umami taste. The spinach acts as the base that brings all these flavours together, and it is nothing short of fantastic! The final dish is colourful and moreish. It's not hard to understand why it is one of the more popular dishes on *zi char* menus. If you've never tried this, we know you'll love it too.

EGG TRIO WITH SPINACH IN SUPERIOR STOCK

Serves 4

250 g (9 oz) spinach

500 ml (16 fl oz / 2 cups) unsalted chicken stock

2 Tbsp Chinese wolfberries

2 cloves garlic, peeled and thinly sliced

1 tsp salt

1 tsp sugar

2 century eggs, cleaned, peeled and cut into wedges

2 salted eggs, hard-boiled, peeled and cut into wedges

1 egg, beaten

1/2 tsp sesame oil

1/2 tsp Chinese rice wine (*hua tiao jiu*) (optional)

1. Remove fibrous layer from stalks of spinach. Rinse and trim into 5-cm (2-in) lengths. Separate stalks and leaves.

2. Bring chicken stock to a boil in a deep pan. Add wolfberries and garlic and boil for 1 minute.

3. Add stalks of spinach, salt and sugar. Cover and let boil for 2 minutes.

4. Add century eggs and salted eggs. Cover and let boil for 1 minute.

5. Add leaves of spinach. Cover and let boil for 2 minutes.

6. Add beaten egg and transfer to a serving plate.

7. Drizzle with sesame oil and Chinese rice wine, if desired. Serve.

The gold standard of *zi char* egg dishes, egg *foo yong* is popular
with all local food lovers. Prawns are used in this dish to give it more depth and bite.
This dish is simple to do and can be whipped up in a jiffy!

EGG FOO YONG

Serves 4

10 small prawns

A pinch of salt

$^1/_2$ tsp sugar

Ground white pepper,
  as needed

5 eggs

1 Tbsp light soy sauce

3 Tbsp cooking oil

1 medium onion, peeled
  and sliced

1 spring onion (scallion), cut
  into 2.5-cm (1-in) lengths

Coriander leaves (cilantro)

1. Clean, peel and devein prawns. Cut into small pieces, then season with salt, sugar and $^1/_4$ tsp pepper. Mix well.

2. Crack eggs into a bowl, then season with light soy sauce and $^1/_4$ tsp pepper.

3. Heat 1 Tbsp oil in a wok over medium heat. Add onion and stir-fry until onion starts to turn translucent.

4. Add prawns and stir-fry until prawns start to change colour. Remove from heat and add mixture to beaten eggs. Add spring onion and mix well.

5. Reheat wok with 2 Tbsp oil. Turn heat to high and make sure wok is evenly coated with oil. Once wok is hot, turn heat down, add egg mixture and swirl wok to spread egg out evenly.

6. Using a wok spatula, turn and gently push edges of cooked egg towards the centre. Let egg cook and set, then swirl the wok and flip the omelette. Let cook until omelette is golden brown on both sides.

7. Dish out, garnish with coriander and serve.

Many believe that the use of a hotplate is simply for the visual factor.
Perhaps so, but no one can deny the fact that the SIZZLING of the eggs
and spicy bean paste on the hotplate triggers all your senses! Now dig in!

HOTPLATE TOFU

Serves 4

2 tubes egg tofu,
  each 150 g (5$\frac{1}{3}$ oz)

Cooking oil as needed

30 g (1 oz) ginger, peeled
  and chopped

20 g ($\frac{2}{3}$ oz) garlic, peeled
  and chopped

50 g (1$\frac{3}{4}$ oz) carrot, peeled
  and sliced

50 g (1$\frac{3}{4}$ oz) canned button
  mushrooms, sliced

1 Tbsp sugar

1 tsp salt

$\frac{1}{2}$ tsp ground white pepper

10 medium prawns, peeled
  and deveined

1 Tbsp cornflour, mixed
  with 2 Tbsp water

2 eggs, beaten

1 spring onion (scallion),
  chopped

MINCED MEAT

150 g (5$\frac{1}{3}$ oz) minced pork

1 tsp sesame oil

$\frac{1}{4}$ tsp salt

$\frac{1}{4}$ tsp ground white pepper

1 tsp light soy sauce

1 tsp cornflour

SAUCE

2 Tbsp oyster sauce

2 Tbsp chilli bean paste

1 Tbsp light soy sauce

1 Tbsp Chinese rice wine
  (hua tiao jiu) (optional)

125 ml (4 fl oz / $\frac{1}{2}$ cup) water

1. Prepare minced meat. Combine ingredients for minced meat in a bowl and mix well. Set aside to marinate for 10 minutes.

2. Cut each tube of tofu into 5 sections.

3. Heat sufficient oil for deep-frying in a wok over medium heat. Add tofu and deep-fry until golden brown. Drain and set aside.

4. Prepare sauce. Combine oyster sauce, chilli bean paste, light soy sauce, Chinese rice wine, if desired, and water in a bowl. Mix well and set aside.

5. Heat 3 Tbsp oil in a pan over medium heat. Add ginger and garlic and stir-fry until fragrant.

6. Add minced meat and stir-fry lightly.

7. Add carrot and mushrooms and mix well.

8. Add sauce and bring to a boil. Season with sugar, salt and pepper.

9. Add prawns and cook for about 3 minutes until prawns are done.

10. Add cornflour mixture and mix well. Simmer until sauce thickens.

11. Place hot plate on stove to heat up. When hot, brush hot plate with 1 tsp oil. Pour beaten egg onto hot plate, then top with fried tofu. Spoon minced meat mixture over. Garnish with spring onion and serve.

A clay pot will help retain heat and keep the food bubbling hot while maintaining the flavours, as opposed to a furiously sizzling hot plate. The key to making a good clay pot tofu is to use pressed tofu that will retain its shape even after frying.

CLAY POT TOFU

Serves 4

6 dried shiitake mushrooms

Cooking oil for deep-frying

300 g (11 oz) pressed tofu, cut into 8 pieces

Water, as needed

1 tsp salt

40 g (1^1/$_3$ oz) carrot, peeled and sliced

8 snow peas

20 g (^{2}/$_3$ oz) ginger, peeled and sliced

1 Tbsp minced garlic

150 g (5^1/$_3$ oz) roast pork belly, thickly sliced

Coriander leaves (cilantro)

SAUCE

1 Tbsp light soy sauce

1 Tbsp dark soy sauce

1 Tbsp oyster sauce

1 Tbsp Chinese rice wine (*hua tiao jiu*) (optional)

1 Tbsp sesame oil

1 Tbsp cornflour, mixed with 2 Tbsp water

1. Soak mushrooms in hot water until softened. Trim stems and discard. Slice caps into strips. Set aside.

2. Heat sufficient oil for deep-frying in a wok over medium heat. Add tofu and deep-fry until golden brown. Drain and set aside.

3. Prepare sauce. Combine soy sauces, oyster sauce, Chinese rice wine, if desired, sesame oil and water in a bowl. Mix well and set aside.

4. Boil a pot of water and add 1 tsp salt. Add carrot and snow peas and blanch for 3 minutes. Drain and set aside.

5. Heat 2 Tbsp oil in a wok over medium heat. Add ginger and garlic and stir-fry until fragrant.

6. Add roast pork belly and stir-fry until fragrant.

7. Add mushrooms, carrot and snow peas, and stir-fry for 1 minute.

8. Add sauce mixture and bring to a boil. Add cornflour mixture and stir until sauce thickens.

9. Add fried tofu and mix gently. Transfer mixture to a clay pot.

10. Add 250 ml (8 fl oz / 1 cup) water to clay pot and cover pot. Bring water to a boil.

11. Remove from heat and garnish with coriander. Serve.

Chye poh, preserved radish bits, makes an excellent savoury topping for any dish.
Deep-fried, it releases a rich and sweet aroma that puts our salivary glands into overdrive!
This goes so well with the deep-fried tofu that is crusty on the outside and soft on the inside.

CHYE POH TOFU

Serves 4

Cooking oil for deep-frying

150 g (5¹/₃ oz) sweet *chye poh* (preserved turnip)

300 g (11 oz) pressed tofu, sliced horizontally into 2 thin slabs

Water, as needed

1 tsp salt

8 stalks baby bok choy

SAUCE

4 Tbsp water

4 Tbsp abalone sauce

1 Tbsp light soy sauce

1 tsp sugar

1. Heat sufficient oil for deep-frying in a wok over medium heat. Add sweet *chye poh* and deep-fry until golden brown. Remove with a strainer and set aside to drain.

2. Reheat oil and deep-fry tofu until golden brown. Drain and set aside on a serving plate.

3. Boil a pot of water and add 1 tsp salt. Blanch baby bok choy for 2–3 minutes. Drain and arrange around fried tofu on serving plate.

4. Prepare sauce. Combine all ingredients for sauce in a wok and mix well. Simmer until sauce thickens.

5. Pour sauce over tofu and baby bok choy. Top with fried *chye poh*. Serve.

Sambal *kangkong* is a dish that looks deceptively simple as it doesn't require much preparation. BUT, to churn out a good sambal *kangkong* dish, the wok has to be SMOKING hot when the *kangkong* goes in. Cook in small batches and don't be impatient because the moment too much *kangkong* hits the wok, the temperature lowers and your stir-fry becomes soup!

SAMBAL KANGKONG

Serves 4

200 g (7 oz) *kangkong*
(water spinach)

2 Tbsp cooking oil

2 Tbsp water

2 bird's eye chillies (*cili padi*),
chopped (optional)

SAMBAL BELACAN

2 Tbsp dried prawns,
soaked to soften

2 red chillies

5 bird's eye chillies (*cili padi*)
or 2 additional red chillies

3 cloves garlic, peeled

5 shallots, peeled

10 g (1/3 oz) *belacan*
(dried prawn paste)

3 Tbsp cooking oil

1. Prepare sambal *belacan*. Drain dried prawns and place into a food processor with chillies, garlic and shallots. Blend into a fine paste.

2. Dry-fry *belacan* in a wok, breaking it up until fragrant and dry. Add oil and stir-fry lightly.

3. Add blended chilli paste and stir-fry until colour darkens. Transfer sambal *belacan* to a bowl and set aside.

4. Trim roots from *kangkong*. Cut and separate stems and leaves.

5. Heat oil in a clean wok over medium heat. Add sambal *belacan* and stir-fry lightly.

6. Add *kangkong* stems and stir-fry for 2 minutes.

7. Add *kangkong* leaves and 2 Tbsp water. Continue to stir-fry until *kangkong* starts to wilt.

8. Dish out and garnish with chillies if desired. Serve.

Another classic homely dish. The eggplants and minced meat are braised in a tasty mixture of spicy bean paste and soy sauce which they absorb readily, offering a burst of flavour with every mouthful. The salted fish adds yet another layer of aroma to the dish.

EGGPLANT WITH MINCED PORK AND SALTED FISH

Serves 4

3 medium eggplants
(aubergine/brinjal)

Cooking oil for deep-frying

1 Tbsp minced garlic

1 Tbsp minced ginger

50 g (1³/₄ oz) salted fish in oil,
cut into cubes

150 g (5¹/₃ oz) minced pork

30 g (1 oz) spring onions
(scallions), chopped

1 Tbsp cornflour, mixed
with 2 Tbsp water

SAUCE

2 Tbsp light soy sauce

4 Tbsp water

2 Tbsp spicy bean paste

2 Tbsp Chinese black vinegar

1¹/₂ Tbsp sugar

1 Tbsp Chinese rice wine
(*hua tiao jiu*)

1. Trim stem end of eggplants, then halve lengthwise and cut into 8-cm (3-in) lengths.

2. Heat sufficient oil for deep-frying in a wok over medium heat. Add eggplants and deep-fry until lightly brown. Drain and set aside.

3. Combine all ingredients for sauce in a bowl. Mix well and set aside.

4. Leave about 3 Tbsp oil in the wok and reheat over medium heat. Add garlic, ginger and salted fish and stir-fry until fragrant.

5. Add minced pork and stir-fry until pork is cooked.

6. Add sauce mixture and mix well. Bring to a boil.

7. Add fried eggplants and let braise for 1–2 minutes.

8. Add spring onions and stir-fry to mix.

9. Add cornflour mixture and stir until sauce thickens.

10. Dish out and garnish as desired. Serve.

A simple stir-fry flavoured with oyster sauce. This recipe is great for whenever you need a green dish on the dining table. We added shiitake and king mushrooms for that extra bite to go with the greens!

STIR-FRIED BABY KAI LAN WITH MUSHROOMS

Serves 4

2 Tbsp cooking oil

1 Tbsp minced garlic

8 small dried shiitake mushrooms, soaked in hot water until softened, stems trimmed

2 king oyster mushrooms, sliced

250 g (9 oz) baby *kai lan*, trimmed

3 Tbsp chicken stock

2 Tbsp oyster sauce

1 Tbsp Chinese rice wine (*hua tiao jiu*)

1 tsp sesame oil

1 tsp sugar

Salt, to taste

Ground white pepper, to taste

1. Heat oil in a wok over medium. Add garlic and stir-fry until fragrant.

2. Add shiitake and oyster mushrooms and stir-fry for 2–3 minutes.

3. Add baby *kai lan* and stir-fry lightly. Once vegetables start to soften, add chicken stock, oyster sauce, Chinese rice wine, sesame oil and sugar. Stir-fry to mix.

4. Season with salt and pepper to taste. Dish out and serve.

This evergreen *zi char* dish is spicy, crunchy and tasty all at the same time!
The minced garlic goes perfectly with the dried prawns and is fragrant to the core.
Fry it, mix it well and you're done!

FRENCH BEANS WITH DRIED PRAWNS

Serves 4

3 Tbsp dried prawns

300 ml (10 fl oz / 1¼ cups) cooking oil

250 g (9 oz) French beans, ends trimmed

2 Tbsp minced garlic

1 Tbsp sambal chilli

1 tsp light soy sauce

1 Tbsp Chinese rice wine (*hua tiao jiu*)

1. Mince dried prawns as finely as possible. Set aside.

2. Heat oil in a wok over medium heat. Add French beans and let cook until they start to shrink. Remove with a strainer and set aside to drain.

3. Leave about 2 Tbsp oil in the wok and reheat. Add garlic, minced dried prawns and sambal chilli. Stir-fry until fragrant.

4. Return French beans to wok and mix well. Season with light soy sauce and Chinese rice wine.

5. Dish out and serve.

ONE-DISH MEALS

Crab *bee hoon* is a popular dish found on the menus of seafood restaurants and *zi char* stalls all over Singapore. If you're a crab lover, you're bound to love this dish as the *bee hoon* readily absorbs the sweet, flavourful juices from the crabs, making every mouthful a delight!

CRAB BEE HOON

Serves 4

2 mud crabs

4 Tbsp cooking oil

20 g (²/₃ oz) ginger, peeled and sliced

3 cloves garlic, peeled and sliced

¹/₂ medium onion, peeled and sliced

4 Tbsp Chinese rice wine (*hua tiao jiu*)

300 ml (10 fl oz / 1¹/₄ cups) chicken/prawn stock

200 g (7 oz) fine *bee hoon* (rice vermicelli), soaked in water to soften

Coriander leaves (cilantro)

SAUCE

2 Tbsp light soy sauce

1 Tbsp oyster sauce

1 Tbsp dark soy sauce

1 Tbsp fish sauce

1. Clean crabs and remove gills. Cut into quarters. Set aside.

2. Combine ingredients for sauce in a bowl. Mix well and set aside.

3. Heat oil in a wok over medium heat. Add ginger, garlic and onion. Stir-fry lightly until fragrant.

4. Add crabs and Chinese rice wine and stir-fry over high heat for 2–3 minutes.

5. Add chicken/prawn stock and cook until crabs start to turn red.

6. Drain *bee hoon* and add to wok. Add sauce and mix well. Cover wok and let cook for a few minutes until *bee hoon* has absorbed the sauce.

7. Dish out and garnish with coriander leaves. Serve.

San lou hor fun literally means tossing three ingredients together. And in this case, the three ingredients refer to the *hor fun*, bean sprouts and fish slices. The key to a good *san lou hor fun* is in the stock for the sauce. Use a good chicken or fish stock to make this a real winner. Using fresh fish slices and crunchy bean sprouts won't hurt either.

SAN LOU HOR FUN

Serves 4

150 g (5¹/₃ oz) *hor fun/ kway teow*

Water, as needed

200 g (7 oz) snakehead (*toman*) fish fillet, sliced

100 g (3¹/₂ oz) bean sprouts, ends trimmed

250 ml (8 fl oz / 1 cup) chicken/fish stock

1 tsp light soy sauce

¹/₂ tsp salt

1 Tbsp tapioca starch, mixed with 2 Tbsp water

40 g (1¹/₃ oz) spring onions (scallions), cut into 5-cm (2-in) lengths

¹/₄ tsp ground white pepper

1. Blanch *hor fun/kway teow* in boiling water for 1 minute. Drain and set aside on a serving plate.

2. Repeat to blanch fish slices for 1–2 minutes. Drain and set aside on a separate plate.

3. Bring 250 ml (8 fl oz / 1 cup) water to a boil in a wok. Add bean sprouts and let cook lightly.

4. Add chicken/fish stock, light soy sauce and salt. Bring to a boil, then add blanched fish slices.

5. Add tapioca starch mixture and stir to thicken stock.

6. Add spring onions and season with pepper.

7. Ladle stock and ingredients over *hor fun/kway teow* and serve.

BONUS RECIPES

Desserts are hardly served at *zi char* stalls, although some may offer cut fruit on the house. Despite that, we really couldn't bear to leave this all-time favourite out, so we're sneaking it in as a bonus recipe! Shh... Our version of *orh ni* is smooth, creamy and utterly delicious. The secret ingredient is lard that gives the paste its super smooth and silky creaminess. The lard also adds fragrance that other ingredients will not be able to provide!

ORH NI YAM PASTE

Serves 4

100 g (3¹⁄₂ oz) pumpkin, peeled

50 g (1³⁄₄ oz) ginkgo nuts

600 g (1 lb 5¹⁄₃ oz) yam, peeled and cut into cubes

100 ml (3¹⁄₂ fl oz) water

100 g (3¹⁄₂ oz) pork lard

100 g (3¹⁄₂ oz) sugar

4 Tbsp coconut milk, or to taste

1. Steam pumpkin for 15 minutes or until soft. Mash with a fork and set aside.

2. Steam ginkgo nuts for 10 minutes. Remove and set aside.

3. Steam yam for 25 minutes or until soft. Remove and add to a food processor while hot. Add half the amount of water and blend until smooth. Set aside.

4. Melt pork lard in a wok over medium heat. Add blended yam and mix well. Add remaining water and sugar and mix until yam paste is smooth.

5. Transfer yam paste to a large bowl or individual serving bowls. Add mashed pumpkin and coconut milk. Top with ginkgo nuts. Serve.

This is none other than the famous Singapore chilli crab! We featured this recipe in our first book, *Hawker Favourites*, and included it here as a bonus recipe because it is such a popular dish. It is undoubtedly the flavourful combination of the sweet and spicy sauce that makes chilli crab one of Singapore's national favourites.

CHILLI CRAB

Serves 4

2 mud crabs

Coriander leaves (cilantro)

16 fried *mantou* (steamed buns)

SAUCE

5 Tbsp cooking oil

1 tsp *tau cheo* (fermented soy bean paste)

3 Tbsp sugar

1/2 tsp salt

5 Tbsp tomato ketchup

250 ml (8 fl oz / 1 cup) boiling water

2 eggs, beaten

CHILLI PASTE

5 shallots, peeled

5 cloves garlic, peeled

5 red chillies, seeds removed

8 dried chillies, seeds removed and rehydrated in water

1 stalk lemongrass

6 candlenuts

4 slices galangal

1 green lime

2 Tbsp *belacan* (dried prawn paste), toasted

1. Clean crabs and remove gills. Cut into quarters. Set aside.

2. Prepare sauce. Place all ingredients for chilli paste in a food processor and blend into a smooth paste.

3. Heat oil in a wok over medium heat. Add chilli paste and stir-fry until aromatic.

4. Add *tau cheo*, sugar, salt and tomato ketchup. Mix well.

5. Add crabs and mix to coat crabs with sauce.

6. Add boiling water and cover wok with a lid. Lower heat and simmer for 8–12 minutes, until crabs turn bright red.

7. Slowly stir beaten eggs into sauce. Let cook for 1–2 minutes.

8. Dish out and garnish with coriander leaves. Serve with fried *mantou*.

Here's another bonus recipe from our first book
simply because it is such a popular *zi char* dish and you deserve to try it!
Trust us — once you start eating this, it's hard to stop. Enjoy!

BLACK PEPPER CRAB

Serves 4

2 Sri Lankan mud crabs, each about 800 g (1³/₄ lb)

3 Tbsp black peppercorns

1 Tbsp white peppercorns

Cooking oil for deep-frying

60 g (2 oz) butter

3 Tbsp chopped garlic

3 Tbsp chopped shallots

¹/₂ cup curry leaves

2 Tbsp sliced bird's eye chillies (*cili padi*)

3 Tbsp oyster sauce

3 Tbsp light soy sauce

3 Tbsp sugar

100 ml (3¹/₂ fl oz) water

Coriander leaves (cilantro)

1. Clean crabs and remove gills. Cut into quarters. Set aside.

2. Heat a pan over medium heat and dry-roast black and white peppercorns until fragrant. Using a spice mill, grind peppercorns coarsely.

3. Heat oil for deep-frying in a wok over medium heat. Add crabs and deep-fry for 3 minutes or until they turn bright red. Remove and drain well.

4. Drain oil from wok and add butter. Add garlic, shallots, ground peppercorns, curry leaves and chillies. Stir-fry until fragrant.

5. Add oyster sauce, light soy sauce, sugar and water.

6. Add crabs and stir-fry for 5–7 minutes.

7. Dish out and garnish with coriander leaves. Serve hot.

WEIGHTS AND MEASURES

Quantities for this book are given in metric, imperial and American (spoon and cup) measures. Standard spoon and cup measurements used are: 1 teaspoon = 5 ml, 1 tablespoon = 15 ml and 1 cup = 250 ml. All measures are level unless otherwise stated.

LIQUID AND VOLUME MEASURES

Metric	Imperial	American
5 ml	$1/6$ fl oz	1 teaspoon
10 ml	$1/3$ fl oz	1 dessertspoon
15 ml	$1/2$ fl oz	1 tablespoon
60 ml	2 fl oz	$1/4$ cup (4 tablespoons)
85 ml	$2^1/2$ fl oz	$1/3$ cup
90 ml	3 fl oz	$3/8$ cup (6 tablespoons)
125 ml	4 fl oz	$1/2$ cup
180 ml	6 fl oz	$3/4$ cup
250 ml	8 fl oz	1 cup
300 ml	10 fl oz ($1/2$ pint)	$1^1/4$ cups
375 ml	12 fl oz	$1^1/2$ cups
435 ml	14 fl oz	$1^3/4$ cups
500 ml	16 fl oz	2 cups
625 ml	20 fl oz (1 pint)	$2^1/2$ cups
750 ml	24 fl oz ($1^1/5$ pints)	3 cups
1 litre	32 fl oz ($1^3/5$ pints)	4 cups
1.25 litres	40 fl oz (2 pints)	5 cups
1.5 litres	48 fl oz ($2^2/5$ pints)	6 cups
2.5 litres	80 fl oz (4 pints)	10 cups

OVEN TEMPERATURE

	°C	°F	Gas Regulo
Very slow	120	250	1
Slow	150	300	2
Moderately slow	160	325	3
Moderate	180	350	4
Moderately hot	190/200	370/400	5/6
Hot	210/220	410/440	6/7
Very hot	230	450	8
Super hot	250/290	475/550	9/10

DRY MEASURES

Metric	Imperial
30 grams	1 ounce
45 grams	$1^1/2$ ounces
55 grams	2 ounces
70 grams	$2^1/2$ ounces
85 grams	3 ounces
100 grams	$3^1/2$ ounces
110 grams	4 ounces
125 grams	$4^1/2$ ounces
140 grams	5 ounces
280 grams	10 ounces
450 grams	16 ounces (1 pound)
500 grams	1 pound, $1^1/2$ ounces
700 grams	$1^1/2$ pounds
800 grams	$1^3/4$ pounds
1 kilogram	2 pounds, 3 ounces
1.5 kilograms	3 pounds, $4^1/2$ ounces
2 kilograms	4 pounds, 6 ounces

LENGTH

Metric	Imperial
0.5 cm	$1/4$ inch
1 cm	$1/2$ inch
1.5 cm	$3/4$ inch
2.5 cm	1 inch

ABBREVIATION

tsp	teaspoon
Tbsp	tablespoon
g	gram
kg	kilogram
ml	millilitre